SKY DANCERS

by **Connie Ann Kirk** · illustrated by **Christy Hale**

Lee & Low Books Inc. • New York

LEE & LOW BOOKS Inc., 95 Madison Avenue, New York, NY 10016
leeandlow.com

Manufactured in China

Book design by Christy Hale
Book production by The Kids at Our House

The text is set in Perpetua
The illustrations are rendered in gouache

10 9 8 7 6 5 4 3 2 1
First Edition

Library of Congress Cataloging-in-Publication Data
Kirk, Connie Ann.
Sky dancers / by Connie Ann Kirk ; illustrations by Christy Hale.— 1st ed.
p. cm.
ISBN 1-58430-162-7
1. Mohawk youth—New York (State)—New York. 2. Mohawk Indians—New York
(State)—New York. 3. Iron and steel workers—New York (State)—New York.
4. Empire State Building (New York, N.Y.) I. Hale, Christy. II. Title.
E99.M8.K57 2004
813'.6—dc22   2004001885

To my father, my hero—C.A.K.

To my cousin Anne Rutledge Sherman,
and to the memory of her twin sister,
Barbara Rutledge Sherman—C.H.

Holding the trunk, John Cloud felt the rough bark against his cheek as he stood in the tree. Right foot, pull. Left foot, pull. Again he had climbed as far as he dared, yet there was still a long way to go. He tested one foot up on the third branch and pressed some weight on it. The branch bobbed up and down, waving its leaves at no one in particular. No. Not yet.

John Cloud leaned back against the tree trunk and felt its strength and wisdom. It was an old tree that had held many moons between its branches. The tree and Mother Earth and Father Sky would let him know when it was time to go higher.

"Time for supper," Grandfather called. He was an old steelworker who used to build skyscrapers in New York City. He walked out onto the porch with his jackknife and a piece of pinewood. He was whittling a heron.

Papa was a steelworker now, off working in the city. He had so much work that he and John Cloud's uncle, Joe Eagle, lived in an apartment there during the week. They came home to the reservation on weekends. Papa said they were lucky to have the work because times were hard and many people had no jobs at all. Between weekends John Cloud missed Papa and longed to visit him in the city.

"Someday we'll take the train down," Grandfather promised, but so far they had not gone.

Papa and Uncle Joe Eagle liked to build. When they weren't building skyscrapers in the city, they were working on the tribal longhouse or raising the roof for a new floor on their own houses. John Cloud rarely left Papa's side when he was home.

"Hand me up some nails," Papa called, and lowered the bucket down from the rooftop. John Cloud dropped two handfuls of nails from the box into the bucket, and Papa pulled up the bucket again. Sometimes Papa sent the bucket back with a stick of chewing gum or a shiny nickel in the bottom.

"Good work," he'd call down, and smile at John Cloud in a way that lit up the sky.

One evening after supper, Mama took up her beading by the stove and Grandfather sat whittling the tail feathers of his heron.

"Papa and Uncle Joe Eagle have to stay in the city this weekend," Mama said. "Would you like to go see them?"

"Yes!" John Cloud said. He jumped and twirled with excitement.

People are crazy down there," Grandfather warned.
"Everyone running every which way, like leaves in a windstorm."
Grandfather always talked that way, but it only made John
Cloud more curious about the city and how Papa put up
with such a crazy place.

That weekend, John Cloud sat aboard the train with Mama and Grandfather and quietly ate the sandwich Mama had made. He watched a flock of geese race with the train outside the window as the train *rickety-rattled* along the tracks.

Even the ride into the city is fast and noisy, John Cloud thought. But soon he liked the rapid rhythm of the train. It made him sleepy. He woke up only when the train slowed, bobbed, and screeched to a halt inside the station.

The city was like so many noisy, honking geese living on one big island! There were traffic lights where John Cloud thought trees should be, and the many buildings so close together seemed to squeeze the air into long shadows. Shoes knocked and scuffed along the pavement. Police whistles shrilled. Taxis honked. If he'd had the chance to say so, John Cloud would have told Mama that the city frightened him.

Buildings seemed to be going up on every street corner. Cranes lifted swinging beams and steam shovels scooped piles of dirt. When they stopped for a moment at a crosswalk, John Cloud tugged on Mama's sleeve and pointed at a dump truck dropping a full load of dirt into a large hole. Mama smiled and nodded. She knew how much John Cloud liked dump trucks when he saw them on the reservation.

"This way!" Grandfather shouted over the sudden rattling of a jackhammer. John Cloud jumped and covered his ears. Mama rushed into the crosswalk behind Grandfather, and for a moment John Cloud lost sight of her in the blur of people hurrying to cross the street. His heart raced as he turned his head in every direction, searching for Mama and Grandfather.

"Here!" Mama called, suddenly appearing before him, her hand outstretched. John Cloud took Mama's hand, and they caught up as closely behind Grandfather as the rushing crowds would allow.

Finally they reached Papa's construction site. Grandfather said they had to stand outside the fence, but they would still be able to see Papa.

"There, on that cross beam," Grandfather said, pointing. It took a minute before John Cloud could make out his father. Then John Cloud knew it had to be him by his shoulders and his walk. He was wearing his cap and his work belt, and he moved surefooted from one workstation to another, across straight beams and down slanted ones too. His feet looked as if they clung to the steel.

John Cloud had heard that Papa was working on the tallest building in the world, but he had never imagined anything quite this high. The building climbed higher than the other tall buildings around it, as if it were racing them, leaping into the air, daring them to get taller too.

"It's called the Empire State Building,"
Grandfather said, smiling. Grandfather's eyes showed
that he was proud Papa was working on such an important
building. John Cloud didn't even try to wave. He knew Papa would
never see him from way up there. Instead, John Cloud just looked up,
and up some more, feeling as if his heart would burst as he watched his
father dance across the sky.

At the small apartment that night, Mama cooked, and Papa and Uncle Joe Eagle played cards and laughed hard, listening to the funny shows on the radio. Grandfather listened too, whittling the soft pinewood as though he had just spent another long day working the iron.

"How do you do it, Papa?" John Cloud asked. "How do you walk across the sky?"

"Some people say anybody with enough courage can do it," Papa said. "But I listen to Mother Earth and Father Sky. If you trust them, they will hold you in their embrace just as they did our ancestors who built the bridge over the Great River years ago."

Sometime later, back at home, John Cloud felt the rough bark of the tree against his cheek again. He thought he could hear the wise old tree's heart beating like a drum. John Cloud took time to listen to what the tree was telling him.

John Cloud climbed the first two branches. Right foot, pull. Left foot, pull. When he looked up, he imagined the Empire State Building racing him, daring him to leap higher. Before he knew it, John Cloud was already up on the third, the fourth, and the fifth branch! He stood higher in the tree than he'd ever stood before, and he was not afraid.

The sky was huge! It was windier and colder up there. Mother Earth looked smaller and bigger at the same time. John Cloud got his balance, and the sky and Earth shifted into balance, too. He could see past his neighbors' yards into the cut cornfields and longhouse beyond. It made John Cloud wonder what Papa could see from atop the tallest building in the world.

"What do you hear, my son?" Papa asked. John Cloud was surprised to see his father suddenly appear beneath the tree, looking up through its bare branches at his son.

John Cloud's feet had a sure hold of the branch. They were telling him he could walk farther out if he wanted to, maybe even dance. But he just stood there, looking down.

"I'm listening to Father Sky," John Cloud said. "He is kind. I will make you proud of me one day, Papa."

"I hear that too," Papa said, smiling. John Cloud reached into his pocket and tossed something down to Papa. He caught it in two hands and held it up. It was a stick of chewing gum.

Papa looked up and smiled. "My favorite!" he said.

John Cloud climbed down to a lower branch.
Then he turned and leaped into Papa's arms,
catching him by surprise.

"Aya!" Papa said, laughing and setting John
Cloud down on the ground. He tousled his son's
hair and curved a hand around his shoulder.

John Cloud wasn't sure if he would work high steel one day like Papa and Grandfather. Maybe he would do that, or maybe he would drive a dump truck on the reservation or engineer a rattling train into and out of the crazy city. There was time to listen to the music of his heart. For right now, he was content to walk beside his father across the yard and into the house for supper, one step at a time.

AUTHOR'S NOTE

THIS IS A FICTIONAL STORY based on the Mohawk (Iroquois) steelworkers who built many of the landmark buildings and bridges in New York City in the 1930s and 1940s. For many Mohawks, steelworking is a family business that dates back several generations.

In 1886 the Dominion Bridge Company wanted to build a bridge across the St. Lawrence River in upstate New York so trains could cross. In exchange for allowing one end of the bridge on their land, the Mohawks secured jobs building the bridge. They became famous for their good balance and their courage in working the steel high up on the bridge.

In 1907 more than thirty Mohawks were working on the Quebec Bridge, when it suddenly collapsed, killing them all. Since that time, Mohawks have taken these well-paying jobs in smaller numbers per site, spreading themselves out to bridges and other structures all over the Northeast.

During the 1930s and 1940s, skyscrapers were being built at a record rate in New York City. Many Mohawks went into the city to work during the week and returned to their families on reservations in upstate New York or Canada on the weekends. Others established a community in Brooklyn to be closer to their work. Mohawks were involved in building the Empire State Building, the Chrysler Building, the George Washington Bridge, and Rockefeller Center, as well as later well-known structures such as the United Nations Assembly Building and the World Trade Center.

Today bridge repairs and new construction still provide work for many Mohawk families. When the World Trade Center buildings were attacked in September 2001, Mohawk steelworkers, including some who were descendants of the original builders of the Trade Center, came in and cut and removed steel during the rescue, recovery, and cleanup phases.

While some Mohawks discourage the folklore that suggests their people have special talents for high steelworking, proud, young Mohawk apprentices still follow in their ancestors' footsteps. They "boom out" from the reservations to work construction and repair sites in New York City and other areas of North America.